ENTRE RIVE AND SHORE

Also by Dominique Bernier-Cormier
Correspondent

ENTRE RIVE

Dominique Bernier-Cormier

AND SHORE

icehouse poetry
an imprint of Goose Lane Editions

Edited by Sheryda Warrener
Cover and page design by Julie Scriver.
Cover image: *"Polaroid #1"* copyright © 2017 by Samuel Bernier-Cormier.
Polaroid print, 3.5 x 4.25 in.
Printed in Canada by Coach House Printing.
10 9 8 7 6 5 4 3 2 1

Library and Archives Canada Cataloguing in Publication

Title: Entre rive and shore / Dominique Bernier-Cormier.
Names: Bernier-Cormier, Dominique, 1991- author.
Description: Poems. | Includes text in French.
Identifiers: Canadiana 20220405433 | ISBN 9781773102870 (softcover)
Classification: LCC PS8603.E76195 E78 2023 | DDC C811/.6—dc23

Goose Lane Editions acknowledges the generous support of the Government of Canada, the Canada Council for the Arts, and the Government of New Brunswick.

Goose Lane Editions is located on the unceded territory of the Wəlastəkwiyik whose ancestors along with the Mi'kmaq and Peskotomuhkati Nations signed Peace and Friendship Treaties with the British Crown in the 1700s.

Goose Lane Editions
500 Beaverbrook Court, Suite 330
Fredericton, New Brunswick
CANADA E3B 5X4
gooselane.com

Traduire pour me rapatrier
Syllabe après syllabe

[...]

Traduire contre les cendres
Traduire contre les cendres
Traduire contre les cendres

    — Martin Rueff, « Haute-fidélité »

What is an omen if not a translation of the past to fit a new form?

    — Doireann Ní Ghríofa, *A Ghost in the Throat*

Contents

Poems

Prose

Translations

Correspondence

Source

Le tableau : un soir d'août 1755, une cellule
de lune sale où un homme se voile le visage,
noue un bonnet sous sa barbe du soir.
Dehors, une frégate qui porte le nom d'une fleur
dort dans le port. Sa femme l'habille d'une robe,
glisse ses bras dans les manches d'un autre
destin. Elle tresse ses cheveux, chaque mèche
une rime, et lace deux pommes vertes
contre sa poitrine. Les gardes brandissent
leurs apostrophes de feu mais n'entendent que
skirt, skirt. Un pas de pierre, un pas de pierre,
une porte bégaye et il jaillit du Fort
comme un sanglot. Le blé à hauteur d'épaule
et ses jambes récitent par cœur un long poème
de peur. La lune lui traduit un chemin
jusqu'à la rivière. Dans l'eau, la robe éclot,
électrique, et palpite comme un soleil de mer.
Enfin, son souffle s'éparpille, en morceaux
de cristal, sur l'autre rive.
Il essaye de se déshabiller mais même dérobé,
le tissu lui colle à la peau comme une histoire
qu'il connait trop bien pour traduire.

Notes on translation

I used to think this was a book about a disguise, but now I know that it's a book about translation.

In 1755, the British governor of Nova Scotia, Charles Lawrence, ordered all Acadian inhabitants to be deported from the colony. This decision was the culmination of a hundred years of colonial conflict between France and Great Britain for control of Mi'kma'ki, the ancestral homeland of the Mi'kmaq.

The French-speaking Acadians, who over the previous century and a half had developed their own distinct culture, as well as strong bonds with their Mi'kmaw neighbours, had refused to sign an oath of allegiance to the British crown. Many considered themselves neither French nor British and therefore neutral in the conflict.

The word *translation* means *to carry across*. Presumably, a body of water.

Between 1755 and 1763, more than eleven thousand Acadians, out of a total population of fourteen thousand, were deported by boat to the British colonies of Maryland, Massachusetts, Connecticut, Pennsylvania, Virginia, North and South Carolina, and Georgia, as well as to France and Great Britain. A translation of a people from one shore to another.

At least five thousand died from disease, starvation, or in shipwrecks.

In 1755, my ancestor Pierrot Cormier, twenty-two at the time, was living with his wife, Nanette, in Jolicoeur, on the Isthmus of Chignecto. In early August of that year, he was summoned by the British to Fort Beauséjour. There, he was read a royal proclamation, declaring him a traitor to a distant crown, and jailed in the barracks to await deportation.

According to family lore, the night before his departure to Georgia aboard the frigate *Violet*, Pierrot Cormier escaped from Fort Beauséjour by wearing a dress Nanette had smuggled into his cell.

If it weren't for that dress, my father always said, we might be speaking English and living in Louisiana, where many Acadians, including Pierrot's brother, ended up settling after the deportation, and where their descendants eventually became known as Cajuns.

In May 2019, my father and I travelled to Lafayette to explore that future we barely missed, ce destin qui nous a effleuré, and find traces of ourselves. To measure the space between two fates, entre évasion et exil.

But still, I wonder: does any of it matter? Was Pierrot's escape in vain if, 266 years later, I am writing this in English anyway, and not in French? Does translation catch up to us all, inevitably?

Despite what it looks like, this book isn't written in English. This is a translation, interrompue. A text stuck entre deux langues, two shores,

a dark harbour où un navire fait escale between tongues.

De : Michel Cormier
À : Dominique Bernier-Cormier
Sujet : Lettre à Dominique

Cher Dominique,

I feel so strange writing to you in this language we never speak, Papa.

This is the opening sentence of your first book of poetry. I sense in these words not so much an apology as an acknowledgement of the strangeness of offering us a book written in English, a language we only speak in the company of friends or loved ones who are not comfortable in French.

English, as you remarked, was for you but a torrent of incomprehensible words when the events you write about happened. You recall how, sitting on the couch, you would see me reporting in English on television and had to ask your mother to translate.

I had never realised, until you wrote this, that, in a way, I had been speaking at you in English during those times.

A Future Dont On Se Souvient Déjà
Lafayette, Louisiana

A guard welcomes us to earth
with an accent and a gun. He runs

his fingers through our clothes,
fifty stars in his mouth, and sentences

my father to a scan. X-rays march
through his bones,

a slow legion de fantômes.
The guard asks us why we're here.

I'm writing a book.
He looks at me, suspicious. *About what?*

Family history, I say.

And I'm his driver, my father jokes.
He waves us through.

As we step outside, the heat hits us
like a future dont on se souvient déjà.

*About transplanting a language
to a new shore, about the roots
it grows in dark hulls.*

Première aube and already
the greenish rumours of tornadoes.

I get woken up at dawn by a weather
alert on my phone.

In the yard of the Airbnb we're renting,
magnolia flowers line the ground

like fossils, bone bright, and fill with rain
that smells like lemons

and scares me.

I turn on the radio, searching
for a Cajun voice that'll click into my chest

like the long-lost half of a twin amulet,
and map our itinerary for the day.

On the futon, my father is asleep,
a book about black holes on his chest.

I record a minute of storm
and slow it down, trying to hear

each drop, but I can't tell where
one word ends et l'autre commence.

Why am I here again?

Even the weather, here, une langue étrange.

Warning signs: funnel clouds, an emerald
tint to the sky, a wind that dies too fast.

Center for Cajun Folklore, I-99
till Breaux-Bridge. Alexandre Mouton house
and Johnny Silver at La Poussière.

To subtitle the rain.

I book a swamp tour online,
but the French boat is full. Instead, a man

with a Hawaiian shirt,
a silver goatee, and a Southern drawl
steers us smoothly through the bayou.

The cypresses grow straight out
of the water, their gothic roots

like tendons in wrists. The tinsel
curtains of Spanish moss

part in slow motion for us
and we sink deeper into that strange, quiet

underworld. Purple hyacinths, endless,
litter the surface like discarded pompoms

in the quiet after a game.

The French boat is out of sight now
but leaves a wake, little fragments of voice

that drift like oil in the water
and disappear, just out of reach.

Every ninety minutes, Louisiana loses
a football field's worth of land
due to erosion.

ces racines-là ça s'appelle des genoux
quand j'étais p'tit
                on les coupait   ouais
on nettoyait l'écorce
                 pour faire des lampes
                              des belles lampes

At the Blue Moon for the Zydeco Jam
and two-for-one Ragin' Cajuns, I push

the saloon doors open
and walk into a poem about the South:

The bartender hears us speak French
and asks where we're from. He uncuffs

his sleeve to reveal an Acadiana flag
and his last name, Landry, tattooed on his wrist.

The bar fills, slowly, and people are drawn
to the soft flame of our speech.

Their fingers rest lightly on the edge
of their glasses like believers

at a séance: G&Ts gliding on their own,
full of neon, across the wet counter,

and am I the medium here?

Un foot dans ce monde
et un pied in the other.

As if I could speak across the veil,
but to what? Leur passé or their future?

The band playing "Tennessee Whiskey,"
a washboard reflecting the blue glow
of a Coors sign.

I don't speak it, but my mémère did.
Just childhood words: étoile, pomme, feu.
I can't remember. How do you say bird again?

At lunch, Mrs. Mavis Arnaud, born
and raised in Arnaudville, Saint-Landry Parish,

makes quick work of a smothered pork chop
and a subjonctif. She explains that

but what can you do?

Six retirees sharing childhood memories
around a teapot every Tuesday

against the crystal canons of English,
against whole battalions of rain. She drives us around

in her Civic, saying the town is green now —
the walls of her house painted

with lime, milk, and local clay:

Going past J.M. Morrow's, Mrs. Mavis
tells me about her husband's body.

How it remembered the great clouds
of Orange long after qu'il ait appris à oublier.

Her voice clear as day.

How a storm can still stir in you
après toutes ces années d'accalmie.

Cajun French is eroding, qu'il se fait gruger
comme la côte par la mer, qu'il faut le protéger.

Non-toxic, biodegradable,
pis tu peux le flusher straight down the drain.

Once a week, Mrs. Mavis leads a French Hour
for the residents of J.M. Morrow's.

We sit at a plastic fold-out table
and my father, ever the journalist, sets to work,

speaking to them, tuning the radio dial
between languages, through that static dusk,

until he hits the right frequency,

and their voices suddenly pour out
claires comme l'enfance.

C'est leur langue maternelle,
mais c'est tellement loin. It's buried
so deep in them.

Vous buviez-tu du Hadacol,
vous, dans le temps ?

Oh ouais. Ça venait dans des caravanes,
ça, tout un medicine show   pis ça vendait de tout
tu te rappelles-tu Yvette
            des boutons   pis des chemises
pis des soldats de plomb
                        ouais pis du Hadacol.

Afterwards, Frank takes me outside
to teach me how to prune okra

before it bolts, French spilling out
of its allotted hour.

As if it worked like that anyways,
as if you could set a language

on a timer switch, like a porch light,
and walk away.

As we step through the glass doors
onto the terrace, the heat still a heavy

cloth, it could be dawn or dusk.

L'heure à laquelle une chose
becomes another.

Regarde ben, là, il faut couper la tige
le plus tôt possible. Il faut prédire la fleur
pis la couper avant même qu'elle existe.

Inside the gates of the Opelousas Cemetery,
my father and I split up, each claiming

a half, searching for Pierrot's brother,

for dates that straddle disaster. My eyes
drift over names, les seuls mots impossibles

à traduire, and I wonder what it's like
de naître dans un climat

and die in another. No luck.

But on our way back, we stop
at a used bookstore where my father is visited

by his mother's ghost. I find him frozen
in the Acadian history aisle,

holding her book. Ses mots
soudainement dans sa paume,

two thousand miles from home:

Sa voix qui surgit du passé,
like snow in the middle of a Louisiana day,

across a whole continent of language.

Joseph Cormier, dit de l'Acadie
1740 (Beaubassin, Nouvelle-Écosse)
1795 (Opelousas, Louisiane)

Cocagne: 225 ans d'histoire
par Flora Cormier

In the Future
Wing of the Lafayette Science Museum,

I summon my very first tornado.

I push a button
and the air inside a glass wardrobe

weaves itself into a dress of wind.

Next to it, an apocalyptic panel:

I hit the button, encore et encore,
trying to pinpoint le moment précis

quand rien devient air and air
becomes ruin,

silence musique and music
song, quand tu te mets à rêver
in a new tongue —

the exact moment
quand terre devient land and land

becomes ocean.

*Extreme weather events will only worsen
in Louisiana, speeding up coastal erosion.*

*By 2100, 90% of Louisiana
will be underwater, swallowed by the Gulf*

I head to the Past and find my father
in an old ship's hull. The sound

of creaking boards plays on speakers
and an ethereal voice whispers

mais Papa est déjà long gone,

sleeping through his own personal Deportation,
la mélancolie en surround sound,

parce qu'on la connait l'histoire,
we've heard it all before,

yeah yeah we know so I wake him up

et on va boire deux bonnes
Ragin' Cajun froides au Blue Moon
et raconter des blagues qui se traduisent pas

parce que le passé
il rejoue une fois à l'heure anyway.

I am the voice of Acadia,
listen to my story of long ago

scattered to the winds of destiny
and doom, bound together by blood

I sit on the porch under the magnolia,
scanning the sky for the hazy green tint

of a poem. I write a line about water hyacinths,
their purple veil, then delete it. Backspace

till all that's left is water, still. My father
comes out with two beers, sits next to me.

I want to tell him I don't always pick
when I write or what I write about,

that more often than not, the page
is a sky waiting for weather.

I wanted so badly to find a perfect
metaphor for language here,

one that would illuminate the fate
of French, forecast if the future was

éclaircie or storm.

Twilight now, nuit et jour
tissés ensemble for a moment.

I drink the last sip of my beer.

Pis, comment ça va, les poèmes ?
As-tu trouvé ce que tu cherchais ?

Je sais pas. Je sais pas
ce que je cherchais. Une réponse, une vision.

Et ?

Je sais pas. Oui et non,
j'ai deux réponses dans la gorge.

De : Michel Cormier
À : Dominique Bernier-Cormier
Sujet : Lettre à Dominique

My initial reaction at holding your book in my hands was one of immense pride at your accomplishment but also of haunting guilt at feeling responsible for the conditions that led you to write it in English.

This is a wrenching feeling, not because writing in English is a bad thing. But I wondered, in our desire to expose you to a wider world, had we, your mother Anne and I, inadvertently created the conditions that made it harder for you to write and publish in French?

The roots of this malaise run deep. For many Acadians, as well as for other francophones, adopting English as one's main language amounts to more than assimilation, it is tantamount to abdication to the language of the conqueror.

You know the family lore well. Our ancestor Pierrot avoided deportation by escaping from a British army prison disguised as a woman; otherwise we could have ended up as Cajuns in Louisiana.

Hybrid/e

The bayou is an armurerie d'argile
where blades of sun aiguisent leur feu

Each night j'attache un ruban
de soie around ma mâchoire

in surrender

and listen to the soft slang de mon sang
whispering in my veins

the sweet nothings que dusk
me chuchote à l'oreille

Fossé | Rift

Le tableau : un soir d'août 1755, une cel   l cell
de lune sale où un homme se voile le
noue un bonnet sous sa barbe du so   dow.
Dehors, une frégate qui porte le   er
dort dans le port. Sa femme l'h   ses him,
glisse ses bras dans les man   a different
destin. Elle tresse ses che   ck
une rime, et lace deux   apples
contre sa poitrine   rds brandish
leurs apostro   mes but hear only
skirt, ski   one, a step of stone,
une po   e bursts from the Fort
comm   p to his neck
   e by heart a long poem
   on translates him
   river. In the water, the dress blooms,
   nd pulses like a jellyfish.
   his breath scatters in crystal shards
   e other shore.
   ries to undress, but even freed,
   e fabric sticks to his skin like a story,
   oo familiar to translate.

Notes on translation

For a long time, I experienced bilingualism as a rift within myself.

To live in two languages is to constantly translate yourself. And translation is an inherently violent process: a forceful cleaving of meaning from words, a ripping of sense from its home.

In this way, Pierrot's imprisonment in August of 1755 was also a translation. Into the jail of English. *Maison* into *fire*, *ciel* into *cell*. Gripping the black bars of sounds he couldn't pronounce. The syntax of his home burning in the night.

But if his jailing was a translation, his escape must be a translation as well, back towards his home language. Meanings freed, for a moment, from the shackles of words, running through a field of moonlight, fantômes without shells, liberated.

A hallway only half lit by torches. Pierrot remembering how the word *lune* glowed dans le ciel, le mot *rosée*, sous ses pieds.

Self-Portrait as Sainte Bernadette de Lourdes

I speak the language of borders and visions.

Occitan: a hybrid tongue, a missing link

in the fossil record between Spanish and French.

My speech a dark cave to them

until a word they recognize flashes its lightning

and they flinch, shocked at the expanse

it reveals, the unseen depth of me, the cathedral

ceilings. Of course they didn't believe me, little cleaning girl,

when I told them I saw uo petito damizelo

in a blue belt at the grotto, with two gold roses

at her feet. They called me either halfwitted

or two-faced, too simple or duplicitous.

Either a dreamer or a liar.

A man with a face like marble sat me down

in a room suddenly both too big and too small

and told me to cut the shit, that I was not chosen,

that secret words did not reveal themselves to me,

their bright petals shimmering at my dirty feet;

told me to unsow the hope I had sown

in the hearts of asthmatic blacksmiths,

that femurs, ma belle,

did not heal faster than sunsets;

told me, with his throat of marble,

that I would not go back to the grotto

to kneel in the blue mud again and cry,

my doubt suddenly dislocated from me

like a shoulder and pulsing limp at my side,

aqueró, aqueró;

but what choice did I have?

I went back and crossed the threshold.

The world split for me, encore et encore,

una y otra vez.

On Young Thug, Mumble Rap, and the Future of Language

Lately, I have been dreaming of another dress. On the cover of his 2016 album *Jeffery*, Young Thug is a wearing a gorgeous periwinkle gown by Italian designer Alessandro Trincone. When he first saw it, he said, he thought God had sewn it for him. The dress a blend of Marie Antoinette and Raiden from *Mortal Kombat*, a union of silk and volts. He had it flown from Trincone's workshop in Milan to his studio in Atlanta. I imagine the dress flying west, drenched in a ten-hour sunset. Rushing through the sky, a violet dream, towards a body born to wear it.

Like a voice wears a throat.

⋮

In many ways, I am not quite Acadian. My brothers and I were the first Cormiers in twelve generations, since Thomas Cormier in 1636, to be born outside of l'Acadie. I didn't grow up there, either, although I spent every summer of my childhood in Cocagne. Perhaps most obviously, I don't have an Acadian accent when I speak French. For those reasons, I'm not always *read* as Acadian, and don't always feel at ease in my Acadian identity.

And yet, in my knack for exile and my hybrid tongue, I *feel* Acadian.

⋮

Young Thug's style of rapping is often called mumble rap or post-verbal rap. As Chris Richards put it in "A Loss for Words: Listening to the Post-verbal Brilliance of Young Thug," he "mangles his words in mumbles, swallows them in yawns, annihilates them in growls." The words blend into each other, a tangled knot of sounds. His voice split by lightning; the bright splinters of a falsetto scattered across a dark lawn. For Young Thug, meaning is subordinate to sound, logic subordinate to dream.

⋮

Today, most of the Acadian diaspora lives outside of l'Acadie. To feel Acadian, then, is often to feel distanced from it.

Perhaps I have never been more Acadian than when I write about it from here, in Vancouver, on the other side of the country, mon regard posé sur un autre océan.

Gérald Leblanc, « Vancouver avec tes yeux » : *j'écris partout qu'est-ce que ça veut dire venir de nulle part   and to love you there and everywhere   à partir de là.*

⋮

Where my family is from, people speak Chiac, a blend of Acadian French and English, unintelligible to the majority of both French and English speakers. Today, linguists flock from all over the world to study it: the unique ways in which it blends the grammar and syntax of both languages; the way their threads are so interwoven.

But to my father, growing up, Chiac was a jail he couldn't escape. Neither, not both. When he left l'Acadie, he spent years undoing that braid of language, carefully untangling his tangled tongue until the two languages stood on their own, on separate shores, perfectly clear.

I am, in a way, on the return journey my father took back then. I am trying to braid my languages back together, to tangle my untangled tongues. To find a language that feels like home, that doesn't split ma langue en deux.

⋮

Young Thug believes he's an oracle. That whatever he raps will come true, that his lyrics predict the future. From the Latin *orare, to speak*: as far back as the second century BCE, "frenzied women through which the gods speak."

⋮

We often romanticize unintelligibility. When I first listened to Young Thug, I was thrilled by the verbal chaos of it, intoxicated by an English that felt just out of reach. An accidental poetry, an apocalypse of words. I fetishized its foreignness.

When French or Québécois tourists visit our part of l'Acadie, they come in order *not* to understand: they are looking for an almostness of French. They believe, like I did listening to *Jeffery* for the first time, that they are visiting the outer borders of language, and are thrilled by the few clear words that rise, like crystals, out of what they consider muddled, mud.

This is the wrong way to listen to language that isn't yours. What we call unintelligible is often an eloquence we aren't attuned to, a voice speaking to us from the future.

⋮

According to popular accounts, Pythia, the Oracle at Delphi, was in a state of trance induced by the sulphur fumes escaping from the cracks in the temple floor. She spoke in gibberish, which was then translated into poetic dactylic hexameters by the male priests.

Scholars, however, have begun to challenge this idea. Some believe the priestess spoke out clearly, in her own voice. That she required no translation.

⋮

People often ask me which language I dream in. For a long time, I thought I dreamt in neither French nor English. Now, I think I may dream in both, at the same time.

I need to believe qu'on peut rêver en deux langues and wake up whole.

⋮

Regarding the song "Lifestyle," the internet is split over what Young Thug sings. *Livin' life like a beginner* or *Livin' life like a volcano*. Neither side is right, of course. He is singing both, at the same time. His voice refusing to land on either shore.

Alessandro Trincone, who designed the dress Young Thug wore on his album cover, says he wants to create genderless fashion, to move beyond the either/or.

The three of us, apprentice catastrophes, born the same summer of 1991 in Naples, Atlanta, and Gatineau, connected in a strange fashion.

⋮

There is a discourse I have heard all my life that claims Chiac is a ruin. The crumbling castle of French falling into a sea of English. But to me, Chiac is a living thing, growing gills, a voice from the future, prophetic and clear.

The future is hybrid.

⋮

On Hajar Benjida's Instagram account @YoungThugAsPaintings, each post consists of a classical scene next to a photo of the rapper.

The similarities are uncanny and graceful: a pose, a line, a fold of fabric. His body hiding behind every canvas, shape-shifting through centuries.

A Moroccan bazaar. A divine clamshell. Versailles. An English orphanage.

For one of her shows, Benjida layered hundreds of semi-transparent copies of each piece in the frame, so people could rip them off, like pages of a calendar, and take them home as souvenirs. When Young Thug walked through, he stopped in front of his favourite one: *Man and Boy in Algiers* (1887), by Anders Zorn — a man leaning on the edge of a terrace, looking out to sea.

Flipping frantically through his own face, trying to reach the original.

⋮

At our cottage on Cap de Cocagne, where the cliff falls, year by year, into the sea, I find a book from 1928, its pages crumbling: *Le parler franco-acadien et ses origines*, par Pascal Poirier.

In it, Poirier pokes fun at the puritan attitude of those who see, in anglicisms, the death of the French language in Acadie. Using *cup*, for example, instead of *tasse*. Poirier points out, with a wink, that *cup* is originally a word that English borrowed from French.

Words that set off at sea, long ago, headed for a distant shore, come back to us in unexpected ways.

Gérald Leblanc : *on passera d'une langue à l'autre / dans la même langue / and wonder what next*

⋮

In my dream, Young Thug appears to Pierrot in his cell, a hologram of hope. Singing in a language from the future. Ruffles the colour of dusk cascading from his waist, a castle of silk, crumbling. Inked across his chest, words that don't exist yet. Around his wrists, diamonds whose atoms are still arranged in dark equations of carbon.

Pierrot can't understand the words, but the message is clear: *fit your fate into a new form.*

In my dream, I walk around an orchard voilé de brume, cueillant des mots tombés d'arbres that haven't been planted yet.

Hybrid/e

Comme je disais, the important thing
is savoir se fendre

le cerveau in half

et de continuer à parler
devant a foule of light

even ébloui, even aveuglé

même quand the vase of the moon
se fracasse dans le ciel

et que la mer again
comme un orfèvre must fix it

and all its little pieces

De : Michel Cormier
À : Dominique Bernier-Cormier
Sujet : Lettre à Dominique

I have meant for some time to respond to you. I felt interpellé by your first line, where you say how strange you feel writing in English.

(Interpellé is one of those French expressions that needs a number of words to properly render in English. It can be translated as singled out, called upon, summoned, prodded, or in the case of arts or literature, inspired. It encompasses a whole range of usages, from being hailed by a police officer, challenged in a debate or touched by the sight of a sunset.)

I too feel strange writing to you in this language we never speak.

Rive | Shore

Le tableau : un soir d'août[1] 1755, une cellule
de lune sale[2] où un homme se voile[3] le visage,
noue un bonnet sous sa barbe du soir.[4]
Dehors, une frégate qui porte le nom d'une fleur
dort dans le port.[5] Sa femme l'habille d'une robe,
glisse ses bras dans les manches d'un autre
destin. Elle tresse ses cheveux, chaque mèche[6]
une rime, et lace deux pommes vertes
contre sa[7] poitrine.

———

The scene: an August night, 1755, a soiled cell
of moonlight where a man veils his face,
ties a bonnet under his five o'clock shadow.
Outside, a frigate named after a flower
sleeps in the harbour. His wife dresses him,
slides his arms into the sleeves of a different
fate. She braids his hair, each lock
a rhyme, and laces two green apples
against his chest.

Notes on translation

1   Written, *un soir d'août* is just another August night. But spoken, it becomes a soft, warm evening: *un soir doux*. Translation, here, denies us the ambiguity, the disguise. It makes us choose, forces us to lift the veil from the word's face and reveal its meaning.

2   *Une cellule / de lune sale* is a perfectly tangled stream of sound (*une/ lule/lune, cel/sale*) but the best I can manage is *a soiled cell of moonlight*, which feels a bit clean, a bit tame — like combing a waterfall, then putting it in a braid.

3   *Voile*: as a noun, its meaning is determined by gender. It holds two different fates, two futures: the masculine *un voile*, meaning *a veil*, meaning *disguise, escape*; or the feminine *une voile*, meaning *a sail*, meaning *ocean, exile*. Here, however, Pierrot's fate is set, it cannot be changed by translation: as a verb, *se voiler* can only mean to veil oneself.

4   *Barbe du soir* becomes *five o'clock shadow*, and I can't tell which I like best. I prefer the figurative *shadow* over the explicit *barbe*, but the general *soir* over the specific *five o'clock*. Still, in both, the time is right: a blue-grey darkness spreading, imperceptibly at first then suddenly there, impossible to ignore.

5   An accidental echo: *dehors, dort, port*. I'm not used to writing poetry in French, and the rhyme is clumsy, obvious. Translation fixes things: *outside, sleeps, harbour*. How nice to slip meanings out of their words and into the clothes of another language, so they can tiptoe by, unnoticed.

6   In translation, we lose the double meaning of *mèche*: both a lock of hair and a wick. (Mayakovsky: *A line is a fuse that's lit. The line smoulders, the rhyme explodes.*) But in the translation to *lock*, we also gain meaning: the poem a door, picked open.

7   In French, the possessive pronoun agrees with the gender of
    what it describes, not the owner of that thing. Unlike *his chest*,
    then, *sa poitrine* reveals nothing about the person's gender.
    In the French poem, grammatically speaking, the guards and
    readers know nothing of the body under the dress. It is only in
    translation that Pierrot is unveiled.

Self-Portrait as the Watercolourist Walter Anderson

Couldn't face one more of them, those gawking pelican vases.

So I left the pottery business for the psychiatric wing of Mississippi State.

Diagnosis: hypothymergasia, undulant fever, fugue states.

From the Latin *fugere*, "to flee."

From the second storey, I made my feverish break: two bedsheets, a good knot, gravity.

On my way down, I held a bar of soap and drew a mural of white birds in flight.

Escaping is an art: to imagine, on your way down, the shape of things rising.

To never leave a trace that rain can't clean.

Later, I made my way to Horn Island, an umbrella for a sail.

Before Carla, a pilot dropped a note from the sky: *Come home, Walter.*

I knew the warning signs: the awful sunrise, the hovering black spirit bird, the man-of-war, just one.

I dipped my brush in the storm and painted the scintillating pelicans.

When the sun shone on the dark feathers, they disappeared.

On the white, they reappeared.

God, we're so small.

After, I visited a meteorologist in New Orleans.

To share what I had learned of weather, of light.

I camped on the levee and woke up to a sound, to colours unknown to me.

An exotic pheasant, escaped from Audubon under a cloak of rain.

We stared at each other, two fugitives.

The sun went down and the bulrushes went to lilac and copper and I rose.

Long after my death, when Katrina hit, my old workshop was flooded.

The Gulf wiping clean my watercolours, erasing its own portraits.

Scrubbing all evidence of itself.

Underwater, the room calm and rearranged.

Jellyfish floating near the ceiling like chandeliers.

And the light pulsing, pulsing, again.

Everything I see now is new and strange.

Hybrid/e

Comme Celan I know
qu'only une lettre sépare *word* from *épée*,

and I wonder comment écrire
dans une langue soiled by darkness.

Become un lac, clair et glasslike?

Ou la bourbe, rising en nuages
pour troubler the surface?

Ce que j'essaye de dire is that I'm trying
to look my myths en pleine face,

the silt of it dans les cils.

Eclipse | Erasure

~~Le tableau : un soir d'août 1755, une cellule~~
~~de lune sale où un homme se voile le visage,~~
~~noue un bonnet sous sa barbe du soir.~~
~~Dehors,~~ a frigate ~~qui porte le nom d'une fleur~~
~~dort dans le port. Sa femme l'habille d'une robe,~~
~~glisse ses bras dans les manches d'un autre~~
~~destin. Elle tresse ses cheveux, chaque mèche~~
~~une rime, et lace deux pommes vertes~~
~~contre sa poitrine. Les gardes brandissent~~
~~leurs apostrophes~~ of fire ~~mais n'entendent que~~
~~skirt, skirt. Un pas de pierre, un pas de pierre,~~
~~une porte bégaye et il jaillit du Fort~~
~~comme un sanglot. Le blé à hauteur d'épaule~~
~~et ses jambes récitent par cœur un long poème~~
~~de peur. La lune lui~~ translates ~~un chemin~~
~~jusqu'à~~ the ~~rivière. Dans l'eau, la robe éclot,~~
~~électrique, et palpite comme un soleil de mer.~~
~~Enfin, son souffle s'éparpille, en morceaux~~
~~de cristal, sur l'autre~~ shore.
~~Il essaye de se déshabiller mais même dérobé,~~
~~le tissu lui colle à la peau comme une histoire~~
~~qu'il connaît trop bien pour traduire.~~

Notes on translation

The Deportation may have been a violent translation — a ripping of a people from their home to a distant shore — but it was not a translation of an original text.

Acadian settlers, by naming the land, had already participated in a (mis)translation of it. The word *Acadie* is a derivation of the Mi'kmaw participle -*a'kati*, meaning "place of."

Acadie, then, is simply a distortion of *here*.

The Deportation was only a translation of a translation, a violence within a much greater violence.

Regardless of whether I write in French or English, I am writing in a language of displacement, of erasure. To insist too heavily on the borders between these languages is to recognize their claims to the land.

The conflicts between French and British powers here were immoral and violent, their claims illegitimate. I refuse to re-enact those conflicts within myself, de signer un serment d'allégeance.

I refuse to believe qu'une frontière armée découpe each bilingual self, je refuse d'être un garde at the borders of language.

LIGO

At 03:50:45 on 14 September 2015, the Laser Interferometer Gravitational-Wave Observatory (LIGO) located in Livingston, Louisiana, made the first ever direct observation of gravitational waves, which Albert Einstein had predicted over a hundred years prior.

To better listen to the gossip of space,
scientists have banished all vibrations
from the region. Dryers are banned

within a ten-mile radius. On our way in,
lab coats hang on clotheslines like chests

emptied of voices. My dad drives too fast

past the *Slow Down, Sensitive Measurements in Progress*
sign and is mistaken for a neutron star
at the wheel of a rented Prius.

In 1994 the United States Congress
signed LIGO into life, to the tune of $395 million.

To build the facility, two hundred acres of land
were "requisitioned," which is another word
for taken. From the Latin *requirere*, "to search for."

What we do here, our tour guide says, is search for
the most violent events in the universe.

We keep our eyes to the sky, ignore
all earthly noise. The very ground

on which we stand. We look
to forces far beyond ourselves.

Before entering the facility, we are asked to silence
our phones and hand over any memories

of eclipses, pro wrestling, and first kisses.
There can be nothing in us that stirs, unexpectedly.

Please don't shake the vending machine, sir.

In a room of screens, our guide explains
that when a star dies, it sends a ripple through the fabric

of space-time. To record it, the lasers
must be shielded from anything else that could alter

their paths, here on Earth. Of course,
there are false positives: a farmer is mistaken

for a black hole
having a heart attack in a bathtub.

A truck, a luminous giant
towing horses in a trailer on the highway.

A text from a loved one,
a bundle of dark matter buzzing in the pocket
of a jean jacket.

Back outside, we stand on a small hill
overlooking a concrete pipeline: from here,

you'd think oil: a slow black sludge,
but instead, light: green needle-blade,

absolute stillness
pumping through that long grey vein.

Suddenly, rain, and we run inside,
our guide swearing under his breath

that a storm wrecks a week of data.
Everything it stirs, unearths.

A rumbling of language above,
scrambling signals.

Roughly 1.6 billion years ago, two black holes
kissed, and on September 14, 2015,

a laser in Louisiana shifted its path
1/1000th the width of a proton — the equivalent

of moving Earth closer to Proxima Centauri
the width of a human hair.

Scientists translated the wave
into a 0.2-second sound frequency,

which resembled the chirp of a bird
and went viral. One scientist even played it

to her mockingbird, who, to this day,
still flutters from branch to branch,

a dead star in its throat.

Self-Portrait as Pythia, the Oracle at Delphi

At night, the world opens its jaws for me

and sings a song of sulphur.

On the seventh day of each month, they come at dawn, walking up the white slope.

Their future like an itch they scratch, festering.

Kings, soldiers, merchants, carrying constellations of coins.

Those who pluck what they want from the sky,

the night their orchard.

More, always wanting more.

They come to me, up the white slope at dawn,

on the seventh day.

Sometimes, I am a laurel and speak to them

through the rustling of my leaves.

Today, I sit on the tripod, its golden legs stretched

over a split in the rock.

Cloaked in smoke, a purple cloth across my face.

They come to me because I speak the language of gods,

because Apollo and I share a tongue.

To translate, I tell them, is to kiss through a veil.

Courant | Stream

Le tableau : un soir d'a[...] night, 1755, a soiled cell
de lune sale où un hom[...] man veils his face,
noue un bonnet s[...] his five-o-clock shadow.
Dehors, une frégate qui por[...]med after a flower
dort dans le port. Sa femme[...]. His wife dresses him,
glisse ses bras dans le[...] sleeves of a different
destin. Elle tresse ses che[...]air, each lock
une rime, et lace [...]o green apples
contre sa poitrine. L[...]ht guards brandish
leurs apostrophes de feu [...]lames but hear only
skirt, skirt. Un pas de pie[...]stone, a step of stone,
une porte bég[...]e bursts from the Fort
comme un sanglot. Le bl[...] to his neck
et ses jambes récitent par[...] heart a long poem
de peur. La lune [...]nslates him
jusqu'à la rivière. Da[...] the water, the dress blooms,
électrique, et palpite com[...] like a jellyfish.
Enfin, son souffle s'ép[...]atters in crystal shards
de cr[...]on the shore.
Il essaye de se déshabille[...]ut even freed,
le tissu lui colle à la peau[...] skin like a story
qu'il connait tro[...]late.

Notes on translation

What does it mean to live in the space between languages?

It is often said that a great poem cannot be translated, cannot be brought across the water, the implication being that its beauty and truth lie in its untranslatability.

What does it mean, then, for a poet to be constantly shuffling between languages, to be constantly translating himself? To cross that border again and again? The space of translation, the moment of translation, is one of turbulence, of shifting currents, allegiances.

After Pierrot escaped, he met back up with Nanette and their children as they fled towards Québec. They lived in exile there for ten years before being able to return to l'Acadie. Having left home but not reached another shore, they were left in transit, unmoored. Stuck in a perpetual state of translation.

Sometimes, I feel like I've left the shore of French but haven't reached the harbour of English yet.

Hybrid/e

Ma gorge glissée through an X-ray

they ask me c'est quoi l'affaire
that lights up the screen

the foreign object
qui fait chanter la machine

Tell us quelle lueur

Tell us quelle fracture

A brain de lilas tristes
and an unquenchable soif d'avenir

De : Michel Cormier
À : Dominique Bernier-Cormier
Sujet : Lettre à Dominique

Growing up in a fractured linguistic landscape did not equip me to realize my burning ambition of travelling the world as a journalist. Even after two university diplomas, one in English and one in French, I did not feel truly comfortable in either language.

My English was sufficiently proficient for news reporting but hardly literate enough for the more sophisticated journalism I aspired to. As for my written French, it still had a formal air about it. As a radio journalist in Montréal, I would run out of breath before I could make it to the end of one of my convoluted sentences. A predicament that was compounded by the fact that the cadence of my Acadian speech made me put the tonal accent on the wrong syllable.

My Québécois bosses at Radio-Canada had given me three months to correct this fault with private voice lessons at the Conservatoire, Québec's national drama school (at my expense). I protested that my speech pattern mirrored the rhythm of the sea, a contention I had borrowed from the Acadian writer Antonine Maillet, but this left them largely unimpressed.

Lines

Lines *(57° 59' N, 7° 16' W) is an art installation by Timo Aho and Pekka Niittyvirta, in which horizontal LED lights are activated by high tide as a visual reference for predicted future sea level rise.*

In a seaside town in northern Scotland

                              an alien blade of light

slices through a stone farmhouse

twelve feet off the ground   stiletto slit

                            horizon of photons

threaded across everything   cows

                      hills   freckled

faces the rainy quiet land   you open

the window of the pub

               and your glass fills with it   and before

you know it

rather than your lager   you are drinking

a pint of catastrophic light   cold down your throat

                        just one more

you say one more and then

            I'm off

but outside there is a bad crease

                of neon across the world

and there is no ironing   no ironing this one

I think   in the distance

                  a cow is sliced in half

by the future   chewing on dark grass

and the water is standing up now in Lochmaddy

its back against the wall   of a stone barn

a notch of light   cut just above its head

in the door frame

                     and the morning mumbling

                                    like a doctor

something about growth

                     about bones   saying

                           this is how tall she will get

Rive | Shore

Les gardes brandissent
leurs apostrophes de feu[8] mais n'entendent que
skirt, skirt[9]. Un pas de pierre, un pas de pierre,
une porte bégaye[10] et il jaillit du Fort
comme un sanglot[11]. Le blé à hauteur d'épaule
et ses jambes récitent par cœur un long poème
de peur. La lune lui traduit un chemin
jusqu'à la rivière. Dans l'eau, la robe éclot[12],
électrique, et palpite comme un soleil de mer.
Enfin, son souffle s'éparpille, en morceaux[13]
de cristal, sur l'autre rive.[14]
Il essaye de se déshabiller mais même dérobé[15],
le tissu[16] lui colle à la peau comme une histoire
qu'il connait trop bien pour traduire.

———

The guards brandish
their apostrophes of flames but hear only
jupe, jupe. A step of stone, a step of stone,
a door stutters and he bursts from the Fort
like a yelp. Wheat up to his neck
and his legs recite by heart a long poem
of fear. The moon translates
a path to the river. In the water, the dress blooms,
electric, and pulses like a jellyfish.
At last, his breath scatters, in crystal shards,
on the other shore.
He tries to undress, but even freed,
the fabric sticks to his skin like a story
he knows too well to translate.

Notes on translation

8 Le rythme de *feu* is not the rhythm of *fire*. I choose *apostrophes of flames* instead, trading a consonance in *r* for three clean iambs, merci bien.

9 An age-old problem: what to do with parts of the source text that are already in the target language? In the French poem, the word *skirt*, in its Englishness, communicates the effectiveness of the disguise: the British guards see nothing unusual here, nothing foreign. One solution is to flip it — *the guards hear only jupe, jupe* — preserving the clandestine aspect of the phrase, the sense of a language infiltrating another.

10 *Stutter* better than *bégaye*, the tongue skipping a step,

11 but *sanglot* better than *sob*, wet blood in the throat.

12 *Éclot* as close to *éclat* as *bloom* is to *boom* — in most languages, so little separating *flower* from *fire*, *fleur* de *feu*.

13 *Shards* lacks the root of teeth, of *mordre* (*bite*) — his breath a crystal glass that shatters in his mouth — but has a sharpness, a needle-blade quality that *morceaux* lacks.

14 As always, I am drawn to the mistranslations, to those words that travel back and forth between languages without changing clothes, fully themselves, doubled in meaning but not in form:

> *rive, rive*
> a shore, déchirée.

15 *Se dérober*: another false friend, a double agent. You would assume: *to disrobe oneself*, especially in this context; but rather: *to sneak away, to slip out*. A perfect little spy.

16 *Fabric* better than *tissu*, carrying with it echoes of fiction (*to fabricate* a story, out of whole cloth), mais *tissu* mieux que *fabric*, avec ses échos d'invention (*tisser* le fil d'une histoire)

and do you know what I mean now quand je me dis déchiré, riven?

Hybrid/e

Les phrases qui poussent in my head
ne fleurissent plus qu'at night

et fissurent a cold floor
dont mes genoux rêvent encore

Les plus belles traductions, like dreams,
sont celles that don't make sense

Fenêtre : to be born on fire
Paupière : a skin of stone

Twenty-nine years now
que j'essaye d'être né

on both sides d'une seule rivière

De : Michel Cormier
À : Dominique Bernier-Cormier
Sujet : Lettre à Dominique

When I visited New Brunswick in the summer, my father would ask obliquely how long I planned to work in English.

At some point, he confided in my mother. I guess Michel won't be working in French anymore, he told her, with a touch of sadness. She, ever the optimist, answered in the way she reacted to most adversity:

Fais confiance à la vie. Trust life.

But that didn't convince him. He was by then sick with cancer, and he would go to his grave believing I had betrayed my sacred obligation to our language.

Self-Portrait as the Bilingual Spy Mata Hari

Believe me, I have always hated war.

Under the blue shadows of palm leaves, my son was poisoned by his nanny.

My husband having killed hers.

I ran to Paris and reinvented myself, as so many have done.

Indian. Javanese. Princess.

My left nipple was bit off by my mustached husband.

And so I covered one half of myself in gold.

I wore these rumours like bracelets around my wrists.

I never told the same story twice.

Once, I danced for the minister of war and he gifted me a horse.

He asked me where I was from and I told him to read the papers.

I told him poetry is a skin-coloured suit.

French men kneeled and begged for my past.

Champagne glasses shattering in their fists, the crystal punctuation of it.

Photographers lined up like a firing squad.

Mountains of magnesium powder on a dark horizon.

I drank absinthe from the mouth of a man who manufactured blue.

We were both factories of colour.

Then the war broke.

The French offered me one million francs to strip Wilhelm of his secrets.

I agreed to flirt with darkness.

I met a colonel of darkness and asked for a meeting with the prince.

To put darkness at ease, I fed it gossip.

Who fucked who, who wore their légions d'honneur to bed.

But the Germans saw right through me.

Behind my back, they nicknamed me H-21, claimed me as theirs.

Grew a legend of me.

Radioed my fake exploits in a code they knew broken.

A dark jewel encrypted in my chest.

It snowed the morning I was arrested in my hotel room in Paris.

Gendarmes walked me down Avenue Foche in their cold jewelry.

Under unbearable light I took off my myths.

Confessed I was born in Holland, told them my real name.

In the papers, they said my body was made to spy.

They held up my makeup case and called it invisible ink.

France loved my foreignness, then hated it.

Despite this, I stood and declared my love of France.

But still they tied a necklace of 50,000 deaths around my neck.

I have always been bigger than myself.

At dawn in those woods, I waited for the flash.

I said no to the veil.

Costume | Disguise

n August n.
ht where a man
et under his five-
frigate named aft
he harbour. His wi
arms into the sleeves
raids his hair, each
d laces two green ap
chest. The guards br
rophes of flames bui
A step of stone, a ste
tters and he bursts fr
p. Wheat up to his nec
legs recite by heart a lo
The moon translates him
the river. In the water,
and pulses like a jellyfish
his breaths scatters in cry
other shore.
es to undress but even freed,
ric sticks to his skin like a s
miliar to translate

Notes on translation

I still haven't quite figured out what Pierrot's escape means to me, what it has to teach me about moving between languages.

If Pierrot's imprisonment was a translation (from the home of French into the cell of English) and his escape a translation back into the home language, then what does the dress itself mean?

The dress could represent English: a linguistic disguise, Pierrot's ability or willingness to wear an unfamiliar language in order to get back to his own; the way a translator must speak both languages in order to translate, to navigate the space between languages.

The problem here is that the dress was smuggled into the jail by his wife, and is therefore a symbol of the home, of the familiar.

Alternatively, it could represent French: a return to the home language, a slipping into the comfortable syntax of its clothes. But Pierrot putting on a dress would not have been a familiar or comfortable experience. It would have estranged him from himself, and in fact, that was the point: to veil his identity, to disguise himself.

The dress, then, in its simultaneous familiarity and novelty, cannot represent either French or English.

Fugitif Chic
Fort Beauséjour National Historic Site

Like someone long dead
or not born yet, the cold voice of the GPS

leads me straight to what remains
of the star-shaped Fort.

At the reception desk, a teenager
pinned to his own polo shirt
by a bronze nametag

says *Bonjour / Hi,*
then asks me why I'm here. I want to say:

Camping, I say. He makes me sign my name
in a book and download an app

that asks me which language I prefer.

As if it works like that, and not the other way
around. As if I don't wake up
every morning afraid

que mon français se soit évadé.

A déjà-vu 263 Augusts in the making.

To check if I've inherited the fugitive gene,
if I can wear dusk right off the rack.

Swaying curtains, an open window
and a note left on the pillow.

Before heading into the ruins,
I ruffle through period clothes for a disguise,

dig through bins of language
drenched in 300-year-old

sunlight, picking words to escape in:

Also: a sleeping pad, a hand-crank
radio and a lantern,

its plastic flame frozen in time.

Outside, I open
the app and point it at the landscape.

On the screen, cars vanish
from the parking lot and ramparts sprout

from the grass, pixel by pixel,
translating the present into the past.

Câline
Mouchoir de cou
Petit corps
Mantelet
Besace

In the tent, I step into my skirt, lace
the ribbons of a falsetto

around my chin.
Comment je me sens ?

Sunset, and the canvas walls
glow like the webbed skin between fingers.

A stiletto slit and through it,
voices in a language I can't pin down.

On the radio, physicists in California
claim to be the first to cut a hole

in the fabric of time. But earlier,
I stuck my face into the faceless

silhouette of an Acadian peasant.

How did it feel?

Did I say that already? Excuse me,

I'm losing all sense of century.

Fugitif chic. Like an oil painting
of a dead forest over which
a bright city was built.

Like lacing the ribbons
of an old voice around my chin.

Evening now and I sit on the ramparts
drinking a growler of Dark Matter

I smuggled past the dreaming boy
at the reception desk. Hypothetical energy

spilling over, a panic of foam
soaking my lap, ma besace, mon petit corps.

South, the Bay is a silver dish
the night slowly unearths with a brush.

The day people are gone. A lone guard
makes his round, patrolling the star.

In the brochure, I read that the Fort fell
the way all things fall:

As the Italians say:
Traduttore, traditore. Translator, traitor.

Une bouche traverse une rivière
et *aube* devient *war*. I turn off my headlamp

et *étoile* devient *dark*.

blueprints unrolled over a table
in hushed tones, a translation paid
in diamonds and future land.

I slip into my FutureLight™
sleeping bag and dream of

Je rêve d'un champ
of blue photons growing across my face,

d'une main smuggling my trembling fear
like a clear jar of moonshine out of my chest.

When I wake up, I can't remember
dans quelle langue j'ai rêvé, the meanings

still whole, not split by the lightning
of language yet. I drift in and out of sleep

for a while, a relief from speech, half-
awake dans les ruines du sommeil.

a woman unfolding a bundle of fabric,
a palm of lune, neatly, the way a cell
duplicates, encore et encore, until
a skin of silk, une silhouette.

In the morning, I change back
into my clothes and fold them, neatly,

the way une main closes into fist,
the way a star collapses into rien.

An employee unlocks the museum.
Cars file into the parking lot. The present

rushes in, a tide slowly rising.
I walk the perimeter of the Fort

one last time and at each bastion
the app buzzes in my palm, reminding me

to stay within reach:

an echo of old
adrenaline, a ghost dans mes os

who still knows to feel fear
when crossing borders, when disrobed.

Stop. You're going the wrong way.

Turn around. Follow my voice.

At the gift shop, I buy a mood ring
in the shape of the Fort.

I cross my name out in the guest book,
a record I was here, then gone.

I leave the clothes
in a neat bundle on the desk,

trying to memorize each stitch, a poem

of fabric, so I can translate it
dans une langue qui tresse ensemble

the different threads of myself.

Can I help it if my favourite
translations are the ones

that don't make it across?

As I walk away from the Fort,

the ring turns the colour
of a sea, indécise, le ciel

a cell left unlocked.

~~Dominique Bernier-Cormier~~
~~August 4th–5th, 2018~~

Se dérober, meaning to undress.

De : Michel Cormier
À : Dominique Bernier-Cormier
Sujet : Lettre à Dominique

For me, writing in French is a visceral process, whereas writing in English is more of a cerebral one. The word *encens*, for instance, awakens a smell; *incense*, its English equivalent, does not.

I don't mean by this that writing in English is a chore or any less satisfying than writing in French. It is, in a way, a lighter experience. My relationship with English words is free from childhood memories and other formative associations. I feel a clarity of mind, almost a clinical distance from the language, that I don't experience when I sit down at my keyboard to start a sentence in French.

I find writing in English strangely liberating.

I like to think that, like me thirty years ago, you are trying to find your voice as a writer, by whatever means possible.

And so, I will make my way home now, reflecting on the strangeness of having written this letter to you in English, and knowing that we will soon be discussing it in French.

With love,

Papa

Le tableau : un ... l'aout 1755, une cellule
de lune sale où un h... ...ne

The painting: one evening in August 1765, a cell

dirty moon where a man veils his face,

ties a bonnet under his beard... d'une fleur

ties a bonnet under his beard... dresses him in a dress, ...

...the sleeves of... and

down to ... a door shutters ...as de pie... green apples ...but hear reddish

...stone step, one stone step

con... ...hear shoulder height... a long poem

et ... ...him ...hatches, ...

...electric, and throbs like the ... of the sea.

Finally, his breath tries to undress but even steals,
of ... electrical, on the other ...ve. ...in pieces

Enfin, son sou... the ...the fabric clicks to his skin like a story

de crystal, sur l'a...

Il essaye de se dés... ...nme une ...

le tissu lui colle à la ... ...nme une ...

qu'il connait trop bien...

Notes on translation

Papa —

To be bilingual, I think, is to discover that words are the clothes of meaning, not the skin.

In that constant translation of oneself, that perpetual back and forth, the first language becomes denaturalized, defamiliarized. It begins to gain more languageness, to become more material:

something to weave and sew.

My proximity to English, my living in it, has made me feel both closer to and more estranged from French. It has made of everything a poem: seen in a new light, à la fois intime et étrange.

Tiphaine Samoyault: *Il faut en passer par la langue de l'autre pour devenir soi.*

I've finally figured out what the dress means.

Pierrot wearing that dress was an act of creativity, of invention. A poem. It represents neither French nor English, but rather our ability to make the familiar unfamiliar again, to move within everyday language in new and liberating ways, to reinvent ourselves.

To stand in the space between exile and home,

entre rive and shore.

Self-Portrait as Pierrot Cormier

Je retire ma voix de ma gorge
like you lift a glass trinket from a shelf

                                    et la remplace par la sienne.

Vision

Seen: an evening d'août 1755, a cell
de lune sale where a man veils son visage,
noue un bonnet under his chin pendant que le soir
grows in blue patches across sa mâchoire.
Dehors, un mot dort in the harbour, a letter away
from violence. Sa femme l'habille, slides ses bras
in the sleeves d'une langue hybride, braids
ses mèches like wicks, et lace une pomme verte
and one green apple against his chest. Guards weld
the night en phrases étanches, with strange
commas d'étincelles. Un bruit, stuck entre
deux langues, breaks l'air. Une porte bégaye
and he dissolves, a drop of blood
dans un verre d'eau. Blades d'or to his neck,
soutirant un poème from his throat. La lune
se traduit un chemin through the clouds.
Dans l'eau, the threads éclosent and close,
éclosent and close. Sa voix, déguisée,
breaks et brille, chaque syllable a bright
cristal qui rime. Il essaye de se dérober,
but the fabric lui colle à la peau
like meanings à leurs mots.

Notes & Acknowledgements

My thoughts about translation, bilingualism, and hybridity were influenced by many writers and poets, most notably Paul Celan, Lydia Davis, Steven Heighton, Gérald Leblanc, Doireann Ní Ghríofa, and Umberto Eco. I owe a particular debt to Tiphaine Samoyault's book *Traduction et violence*, where I first encountered the idea of translation *as* violence, and which helped me put into words many of the things I knew and felt about translation.

The idea of translating (or transforming) a single French poem into a sequence of annotated English versions came from Mónica de la Torre's book *Repetition Nineteen*.

The line "to translate is to kiss through a veil" is a paraphrase of Anne Michaels's "reading a poem in translation is like kissing a woman through a veil," from *Fugitive Pieces*.

"Self-Portrait as the Watercolourist Walter Anderson" uses lines from Anderson's journals (lines 15-16, 27-28, 35) as quoted in the documentary *Walter Anderson: Realizations of an Artist*, as well as quotes from an interview with Anderson's son John (lines 18-20) in Boyce Upholt's "The Many Voyages of Walter Anderson" in the *Bitter Southerner* online journal.

"Costume | Disguise" was inspired by Diana Khoi Nguyen's collection *Ghost Of* and Michelle Nguyen's painting *Ghost Of (Emily Dickinson)*. The outline is based on a reproduction of Emily Dickinson's dress sown by Tania Bukach.

"Tissu | Fabric" was created by putting the original French poem through Google Translate's camera feature and taking a screenshot mid-translation.

This book was mostly written on Mi'kma'ki, as well as on the territories of the xʷməθkʷəy̓əm, sḵwx̱wú7mesh, and səl̓ílwətaʔ, and of the Mississaugas of the Credit, Anishnabeg, Chippewa, Haudenosaunee, and Wendat people. I am grateful to live as an uninvited guest on these lands.

Thank you to Sheryda Warrener for going above and beyond her editing duties, giving shape to my thinking, and knowing what my poetry is about before I do.

Merci à ma famille de m'avoir appris à naviguer la langue avec joie et attention. Papa, maman, Phil et Sam : ce livre est avant tout une conversation avec vous.

Merci à mon père, Michel Cormier, de m'avoir suivi en Louisiane et de m'avoir prêté ses mots.

Special thanks to my brother Samuel Bernier-Cormier for the artwork on the cover, which is a chemically stained Polaroid of the shoreline at our family cottage au Cap-de-Cocagne.

En Louisiane : à Mme. Mavis Arnaud pour son hospitalité à Arnaudville, Barry Ancelet pour notre conversation à Lafayette, Mike le barman et Aaron Thibodeaux pour les bons temps au Blue Moon, et tous les Louisianais pour leurs chaleureux et généreux accueils.

Wela'lin to shalan joudry for her generous comments on the manuscript, and for her clarification on the origin of the word *Acadie*.

Special thanks to Michelle Nguyen for conversations about art, eels, Emily Dickinson, migration, and everything else; and to Annie McClelland for giving me the time to write and travel.

Thank you to the Canada Council for the Arts for their support in the form of a grant, which allowed me to travel to Louisiana and Fort Beauséjour.

Merci à Georgette Leblanc pour ses révisions et commentaires and to Martin Ainsley for his thorough copy editing.

Thank you to everyone at Goose Lane for their trust and hard work: Ross, Alan, Angela, Jeff, Julie, Ben, and Susanne, as well as the icehouse editorial board.

To Kate, who was there from the first word to the last: I couldn't do any of it without you.

In memory of Steven Heighton, who taught me so much about translation, et à la mémoire de Flora Cormier, de qui j'ai hérité l'amour de la langue.

Dominique Bernier-Cormier is a Québécois/Acadian poet, translator, and teacher. He is the author of *Entre Rive and Shore* and *Correspondent*. *Correspondent* was longlisted for the Raymond Souster Award and an excerpt was featured on public transit across British Columbia as part of the Poetry in Transit program. Bernier-Cormier's poetry has also won the Ralph Gustafson Prize for Best Poem and was a finalist for a National Magazine Award, the Montreal International Poetry Prize, and *Arc*'s Poem of the Year Award. He lives in Vancouver, where he writes and teaches in both French and English.

Photo: Kate Balfour